Descendent of
Josiah Lincoln

Descendent of Josiah Lincoln

Susan Mac Queen

ISBN: Softcover 978-1-5035-6445-9
eBook 978-1-5035-6444-2

Print information available on the last page.

Rev. date: 04/21/2015

To order additional copies of this book, contact:
Xlibris
1-888-795-4274
www.Xlibris.com
Orders@Xlibris.com
706590

Contents

This dedicated to my grandchildren and great grandchild to come and my sons

Research

I have added my DNA test results that I took in 2006 that show the result of the SCA5 testing that was done 06/06/2006 that was reported on record. This was done at Hospital in La Mesa California. You may ask what is Ataxia type 5? In my research I have found what it is and I will tell you about it. Ataxia type 5 is a specific type of ataxia among a group of inherited diseases of the central nervous system. It is caused by genetic defects that lead to impairment of specific nerve fibers, carrying messages to and from the brain, resulting in degeneration of the cerebellum (the coordination center of the brain). This information is from the National Ataxia Foundation is where I first started looking into my ataxia. SCA5 is some times called "Lincoln's ataxia" because a 11 generation family with the condition has ancestries that trace to paternal grandparents of President Lincoln.

SCA5 also sometimes called "Holmes ataxia" after Dr. Gordon Holmes, who first described the condition in 1907. The word ataxia means in coordination, of the hands, legs, gait ataxia (impaired balance when walking); and (slurred speech).

SCA5 is a rare genetic disorder, means that it is an inherited disease. This means that abnormal gene is passed along from generation to generation by family members who carry it. Genetic disease like SCA5 occur when one of the body's 30,000 gens does not work properly. SCA5 is an autosomal dominant disease, which means that individuals of either sex are equally like to inherit the gene and develop the disease, and the gene passes from one generation to the next generation. Each child of a person who has SCA5 has a 50 percent chance of inheriting the SCA5 gene.

How is the diagnosis made by a specialist in diagnosing ataxia 5. Is done by a Neurological exam. For me the neurologist did a special blood test that was sent to Athena diagnostics in 200 Forest street 2n floor Marlborough, MA 01752 1(800) 394-4493 or (508)756-2886

That's how I found out I had Ataxia 5, had no clue about my illness or how I was going to live with it and manage it and keep it under control. I will but in this page my result are the American SCA 5 family has two major branches that descend from the paternal grandparents of President Abraham Lincoln. The 11-generation kindred may represent a founder mutation within the US population from my Athena diagnostics medical report. The analytic sensitivity of sequence analysis (direction of a DNA sequence variant, when present, in the gene regions analyzed in greater than 99%. All test results are reviewed, and reported by American Board of medical Genetics certified Clinical Molecular Geneticists. I have SCA5. There are two branches of the family, one is descendent from President Lincoln's uncle Josiah, and another that is descended from President Lincoln's aunt Mary, both of them must of had SCA5ataxia. Josiah Lincoln married Catherine Barlow on February 26, 1801 in Washington County (father of Abraham Lincoln). So Josiah was the uncle and Catherine his aunt. My was born10, May, 1918 and died on 15 November, 1996. I never knew he was my father, I know in my heart he took care of me from a far. For some reason this has been a secret in my family for years, it like the skeleton in the closet that no one wants to talk about. I have traced my father to Barlow Descendents and Allied Families Surname list it links me to the family in the list Crouch Aaron N. 1870 Hendricks County Indiana, and Eliza J Barlow 1845- 1879

Lincoln ataxia is called SCA5 because it is the fifth dominant ataxia gene that was genetically mapped, The gene in the Lincoln family has been mapped to chromosome number 11. The family is critical to this process. To find a gene, blood samples from family members must be collected first, followed by detailed family history, Then DNA is isolated and the gene is mapped to a specific chromosome and then narrowed down to a region on the chromosome. It is time consuming process. If you know that gene lies between point A and point B on chromosome 11, then you have to clone all of that DNA from point A to point B in the laboratory. Then you have to search through all until you find the DNA and it may be millions nucleotides to search through until you find a difference in people that are affected by the disease and people that are not effected by the disease. Dr. Laura Ranum, PH.D., is responsible for the study done at the University of Minnesota. 1994, she liked SCA5 to chromosome 11. She thank the family for participating in the study and made the mapping of SCA5 gene possible. In her study she was ask to research 8 known affected members, after compiling family history, it was found that 35 affected who knew they were related to President Lincoln, they did not know how the disease came down through that connection. I though this was a very good report and very educational,.

Diagnosis Service F

Patient	Requesting Physician	Accession Number 06017750
Date of Birth / Sex F / Social Security Number	Report to	Family Number/Kindred Number
Specimen Type: Whole Blood	Address	Patient Number 999529
Test Category: Not Available	Pathology Department	Specimen Collection Date 04/03/2006
Test Requested: Dominant Ataxia Evaluation		Accession Date 04/05/2006
	Additional Reports to:	Report Date 06/06/2006

Interpretation

This individual possesses one or more DNA sequence variants of unknown clinical significance in one of the dominant ataxia genes **(variant(s) of unknown significance)**. The significance of this new sequence variant may be clarified by careful reconciliation of this molecular data with this patient's clinical symptoms and family member testing if appropriate. Please refer to the Technical Results and Comments sections of this report for further information.

Technical Results

Test	Results	Alert	Repeats
SCA1	Normal		30 and 30
SCA2	Normal		22 and 22
SCA3	Normal		23 and 18
SCA6	Normal		11 and 11
SCA7	Normal		10 and 10
SCA8	Normal		24 and 19
SCA10	Normal		14 and 13
SCA17	Normal		37 and 35
DRPLA	Normal		15 and 11

SCA14 Result: Normal

SCA5 Result: Variants of **Unknown significance**

SCA5 Variant 1: Transversion G > T Homozygous
Nucleotide position: IVS11-7
Codon position: DNR
Amino acid change: DNR
DNA variant type: Variant of unknown significance, homozygous

SCA1 allele 1: 30 CAG repeats
SCA1 allele 2: 30 CAG repeats

Comments

Most Significant result: This analysis identified one or more DNA sequence variants of unknown significance in one of the dominant ataxi genes **(variant(s) of unknown significance)**. Since these types of sequence variants are similar to those observed in both disease-associat mutations and benign polymorphisms, the nature of this variati precludes clear interpretation. These DNA sequence variants, may may not alter the functional aspects of the gene and /or its prote product. While methodologically accurate, the results of this analy cannot be definitively interpreted due to the absence of published studi correlating these variant(s) with clinical presentation and/or patholog Therefore, it is not possible to conclude with any reasonable degree clinical certainty at this time whether or not this variant is associat with the phenotype in question.

Diagnosis Service Rep

Patient	Requesting Physician	Accession Number 06017750
Date of Birth / Sex F / Social Security Number	Report to	Family Number/Kindred Number
Specimen Type: Whole Blood	Address	Patient Number 999529
Test Category: Not Available	Pathology Department	Specimen Collection Date 04/03/2006
Test Requested: Dominant Ataxia Evaluation		Accession Date 04/05/2006
	Additional Reports to:	Report Date 06/06/2006

Possible outcomes: Although the clinical significance of this test result is not certain, several outcomes are possible:

Normal -- the variants are all benign polymorphisms that have not been previously detected or reported and it is very unlikely that these mutations are responsible for clinical symptoms or increased risk of disease.

Carrier -- one of the variants detected is an unreported pathologic recessive mutation, and the individual is therefore a carrier, but such a result is still not sufficient to cause disease symptoms.

Affected -- one of the variants is an unreported dominant pathologic mutation, or two of them are unreported recessive pathologic mutations, and are therefore responsible for the disease.

Uncertainties in the interpretation of these results are due to a lack of documented genotype-phenotype correlations for the variants detected which will only be resolved with further clinical research studies. These results are likely to remain uncertain for the foreseeable future.

Additional test results of less significance: All other test results were within their normal ranges, or were indeterminate. Benign polymorphisms, if identified, are considered normal sequence variants and are not reported here, but are available upon request. Please consult the Glossary for a detailed explanation of "Variant Type" and "Indeterminate" test results if indicated in the Technical Results section of this report.

Course of action for possible resolution: The identified sequence variant(s) may be heritable and/or possessed by this individual's family members. It is unknown whether these sequence variants may lead to, or be causative of, disease. This disorder may be inherited, therefore careful reconciliation of this molecular data with this individual's clinical and family history is highly recommended. Furthermore, testing of this individual's parents and family members is likely to improve the clinical utility of this test result. Athena strongly recommends genetic counseling for this individual and his or her family members, and consideration of testing for family members. Please contact Athena Client Services at 1-800-394-4493 or visit www.athenadiagnostics.com for further information on family member testing.

Other testing available: Athena Diagnostics offers a wide range of other testing services for neurological disorders that have symptoms consistent with a working diagnosis of ataxia. Please contact Athena Client Services at 1-800-394-4493 or visit www.athenadiagnostics.com for more details.

Limitations of Repeat Expansion Analysis: Rare cases have been documented in which young (<20 years of age) symptomatic individuals have one normal repeat and one highly expanded repeat which is challenging to detect.[1] Consequently, these individuals will appear to possess two normal repeats of the same size using the assay performed here. Therefore, if this individual is 1) symptomatic, 2) under 20 years of age, 3) possesses two repeats of the same size and 4) has a

Patient	Requesting Physician	Accession Number 06017750
Date of Birth / Sex F / Social Security Number	Report to	Family Number/Kindred Number
Specimen Type Whole Blood	Address	Patient Number 999529
Test Category Not Available	Pathology Department	Specimen Collection Date 04/03/2006
Test Requested Dominant Ataxia Evaluation		Accession Date 04/05/2006
	Additional Reports to:	Report Date 06/06/2006

documented ataxia mutation in the family, please contact Athena Client Services at 1-800-394-4493 to schedule a consultation with our genetic counselor. In rare cases, extremely large and variable expansions of DNA repeats may not be detected.

Limitations of gene sequencing analysis: Mutations not detected by sequence analysis may include large deletions and large insertions, or mutations in the promoter, 5' and 3' untranslated regions, and intronic variants more than 10 bp from an exon. Mutations in patients exhibiting mosaicism may not be detectable by the technology utilized in this analysis.

Limitations of targeted analysis: These analyses focus on known mutations, or regions of genes flanking known mutations, and usually do not include the majority of the coding sequence of the gene. The analysis of the *SPTBN2* gene (for SCA5) includes the initially published American (Lincoln), French and German mutations (complete analysis of exons 7, 12 and part of exon 14, representing about 10% of the coding sequence of the gene). The residual risk that this individual possesses mutations in the un-analyzed region of these genes is not known.

Background Information: SCA1, 2, 3, 6, 7, 8, 10, 17, and DRPLA are caused by repeat expansion mutations. For conventient and detailed clinical reviews of these diseases, www.geneclinics.org is recommended. The following brief comments cover the more recently discovered, autosomal dominant, non-repeat expansion causes of ataxia. Please consult the reference list at the end of this report or contact Athena Client Services at 1-800-394-4493 if you have questions.

SCA14, or *PRKCG* Mutations: Mutations in the PRKCG gene, which corresponds to the SCA14 locus on chromosome 19, cause nonepisodic autosomal dominant spinocerebellar ataxia.[20-22] The *PRKCG* gene encodes the protein kinase C gamma protein. Mutations in *PRKCG* have been associated with autosomal dominant ataxia.[20-22] Mutations in *PRKCG* may exhibit incomplete penetrance (not all individuals with mutations develop disease) and age of onset within families can vary considerably, suggesting that other modifying genes may influence the development of SCA14 disease.[21,22] Mutations in several other genes including *SCA1, 2, 3, 6, 7, 8, 10, 17*, and *DRPLA* cause autosomal dominant SCA. Mutations in *APTX, SETX, FRDA1* and *POLG1* cause autosomal recessive SCA. In North American populations, approximately 70% of autosomal dominant SCA is caused by mutations in one of the known genes. The relative frequency of mutations in the *PRKCG* gene causing SCA14 is not yet well characterized, but one study indicated that 7.5 % of patients without *SCA1, SCA2, SCA3*, or *SCA6* mutations had *PRKCG* mutations.[22]

SCA5, or *SPTBN2* Mutations: SCA5 patients exhibit MRI and autopsy findings of cerebellar cortical atrophy, Purkinje cell loss and thinning of the molecular layer.[23] A single report documents three SCA5 families with three different mutations within the (beta-III spectrin (*SPTBN2*) gene.[23] The families are of American, French and

Patient	Requesting Physician	Accession Number 06017750
Sex / Social Security Number	Report to	Family Number/Kindred Number
Specimen Type Whole Blood	Address	Patient Number 999529
Test Category Not Available	Pathology Department	Specimen Collection Date 04/03/2006
Test Requested Dominant Ataxia Evaluation		Accession Date 04/05/2006
	Additional Reports to:	Report Date 06/06/2006

German ancestry. The American SCA5 family has two major branches that descend from the paternal grandparents of President Abraham Lincoln. The 11-generation kindred may represent a founder mutation within the US population. The French and German SCA5 mutations, like the American mutation, may be private, familial, mutations, since no additional families have been found to date in these populations. However, since the clinical phenotypes of SCA5 can be mild, these families may be under-represented in research study collections, and relatively large families, though rare, may persist in the general population. Mutations in the *beta-III spectrin* gene are clearly linked to disease and they are likely to be rare (similar to several of the known causes of ataxia).

Methods

General methods for direct testing of repeat expansion mutations associated with ten different ataxias include PCR amplification from genomic DNA followed by high-resolution electrophoresis to determine the number of specific repeats.[1-19] Testing for much larger expansions associated with SCA8 and SCA10 includes Southern blotting and hybridizations using probes.[12-14] Repeat sizes associated with the various ataxias are determined by using one or more of the following three calibration systems: 1. Commercially available DNA standards of known sizes; 2. Athena validated DNAs of known sizes;
3. Internal continuous allelic ladders.

Direct testing for *PRKCG* (SCA14) gene sequence variants was performed by PCR amplification of genomic DNA and automated sequencing of all coding exons (exons 1 through 18). The 4 base pair invariant splice sites (AG ... GT adjacent to the exons) between each of the exons were also examined by sequencing.

Select exon testing for the known SCA5 mutations was performed by PCR amplification of genomic DNA and automated sequencing of only those portions of the gene that contain the known mutations (exons 7, 12, and part of 14 in the *SPTBN2* gene).

Reference sequences for each gene are NM_002739 for *PRKCG* (SCA14) and NM_006946 for *SPTBN2* (SCA5).

The analytic **sensitivity** of sequence analysis (detection of a DNA sequence variant, when present, in the gene regions analyzed) is greater than 99%. All test results are reviewed, interpreted, and reported by American Board of Medical Genetics certified Clinical Molecular Geneticists.

Diagnosis Service R

	Requesting Physician	Accession Number 06017750
Date of Birth / Sex F / Social Security Number	Report to	Family Number/Kindred Number
Specimen Type: Whole Blood	Address	Patient Number: 999529
Test Category: Not Available	Pathology Department	Specimen Collection Date: 04/03/2006
Test Requested: Dominant Ataxia Evaluation		Accession Date: 04/05/2006
	Additional Reports to:	Report Date: 06/06/2006

Reference Ranges for the Autosomal Dominant Ataxia Profile:

Test	Repeat	Normal	Borderline	Full Mutation
SCA1	CAG	≤ 35	a	≥ 47
SCA2	CAG	≤ 31	32 - 35	≥ 36
SCA3	CAG	≤ 40	41 - 52	≥ 53
SCA6	CAG	≤ 18	19 - 20	≥ 21
SCA7	CAG	≤ 18	19 - 36	≥ 37
SCA8	CTA/CTG [b]	≤ 50	51 - 70	≥ 71
SCA10	ATTCT	≤ 22	23 - 699	≥ 700
SCA17	CAG/CAA [c]	≤ 42	None	≥ 43
DRPLA	CAG	≤ 35	36 - 48	≥ 49

a. SCA1 repeats from 36 to 46 are normal if the SfaNI restriction site is present. SCA1 repeats from 36 - 38 are borderline if the SfaNI site is absent, and SCA1 repeats from 39 - 46 are positive if the SfaNI site is absent.

b. SCA8 test results are presented as the number of CTA/CTG repeats due to the presence of a normal polymorphic CTA repeat of size range 3 to 17 repeats located within the PCR product.

c. SCA17 test results are presented as the number of CAG/CAA repeats due to the presence of normal polymorphic CAA repeats having one or three repeats.

DNA sequencing variants are classified as known disease-associated, predicted disease-associated, variants of unknown significance, inconclusive, or indeterminate, or benign polymorphisms. Benign polymorphisms are considered normal sequence and are not reported, but are available upon request. In dominant genes, the finding of a single known or predicted disease-associated mutation is consistent with disease.

Repeat specific methods are required for the following analyses due to unique characteristics of the specific repeat, test technology, or diagnostic criteria. They include the following assay components: SCA1 repeat sizes of 35 to 46 CAG repeats are further analyzed by *Sfa*NI restriction enzyme digestion to identify the presence or absence of the normal interspersed CAT sequence.[2] Southern blot analyses of *SCA8* and *SCA10* repeat expansions are utilized, as necessary, to confirm the absence of expanded repeats, or to verify the number of repeats in highly expanded alleles.[12-14] Southern blotting includes restriction digestion of genomic DNA followed by hybridization with SCA8 and/or SCA10 gene specific probes, and determination of repeat sizes by comparison to known DNA size standards. SCA10 procedures using agarose immobilized genomic DNA for PFGE and Southern blot analyses may be utilized in rare cases, at the client's request, to increase the detection limit for very large ATTCT repeat expansions.

The **size accuracy** of the repeat expansion mutations reported here varies with each DNA and with expansion size. However, when an analysis is reported on a specimen whose repeats are within ± one repeat between diagnostic categories (normal/borderline or

Diagnosis Service Rep

	Requesting Physician	Accession Number 06017750
Date of Birth / Sex F / Social Security Number	Report to	Family Number/Kindred Number
Specimen Type: Whole Blood	Address	Patient Number: 999529
Test Category: Not Available	Pathology Department	Specimen Collection Date: 04/03/2006
Test Requested: Dominant Ataxia Evaluation		Accession Date: 04/05/2006
	Additional Reports to:	Report Date: 06/06/2006

borderline/expanded), the analysis is repeated as necessary to confirm the size using the most accurate methods available in these assays.

For the following SCAs sizing is accurate to ± one repeat, up to the following expansions: SCA1, up to 80 repeats; SCA2, up to 55 repeats; SCA3, up to 85 repeats; SCA6, up to 27 repeats; DRPLA, up to 34 repeats; and SCA17, up to 46 repeats.

For the following SCAs sizing is accurate to ± two repeats up to the following expansions: SCA8, up to 49 repeats and ± five repeats for expansions up to 250 repeats.

For SCA10, sizing is accurate to ± one repeat for expansions within the normal range, to within ± 50% of the repeats for borderline range expansions, and to within ± 25% of the repeats for expansions in the full mutation range.

The **Sensitivities** of these repeat analyses vary slightly depending on the gene, but in general are very high. Current literature indicates that these methods detect the repeat expansions found in greater than 99% of individuals with clinically confirmed SCA1, SCA2, SCA3 (MJD), SCA6, SCA8, SCA10, and DRPLA.[1-7,12-14,18-19] Sensitivity for SCA7 is approximately 98% due to rare occurrences of very large expansions of the SCA7 gene in symptomatic young children.[8-11]
The sensitivity for detecting SCA17 repeat expansions of greater than 46 repeats has not been determined due to the rarity of expansions,[15-17] but characteristics of the test suggest that the sensitivity is expected to be similar to the other genes.

Abbreviations utilized in this report are spinocerebellar type 1 (SCA1), type 2 (SCA2), type 3 (SCA3, or Machado- Joseph disease, MJD), type 5 (SCA5), type 6 (SCA6), type 7 (SCA7), type 8 (SCA8), type 10 (SCA10), type 14 (SCA14), type 17 (SCA17), dentatorubral- pallidoluysian atrophy (DRPLA). Gene names (and associated protein names) are RKCG (protein kinase C gamma) and *SPTBN2* (beta-III spectrin).

Tests are covered by U.S. Patent No. 5,741,645 and 5,834,183 for SCA1, 6,673,535 and 6,844,431 for SCA2, 5,840,491 for SCA3, 5,853,995 and 6,303,307 for SCA6, 6,280,938 and 6,514,755 for SCA7, 6,524,791 for SCA8, and pending patents for SCA5 (SPTBN2) and SCA14 (PRKCG).

References

See www.genetests.com for updated online reviews on many of these diseases and molecular tests.

Review:
1. Zoghbi, H. (1997) AAN 49th Annual Meeting, Course 112

SCA1:
2. Orr, H.T. et al. (1993) Nature Genetics 4: 221-226

Diagnosis Service Rep

	Requesting Physician	Accession Number 06017750
Sex Social Security Number	Report to	Family Number/Kindred Number
Specimen Type Whole Blood	Address	Patient Number 999529
Test Category Not Available	Pathology Department	Specimen Collection Date 04/03/2006
Test Requested Dominant Ataxia Evaluation		Accession Date 04/05/2006
	Additional Reports to:	Report Date 06/06/2006

SCA2:
3. Pulst, S.-M. et al. (1996) Nature Genetics 14: 269-276
4. Geschwind, D.H. et al. (1997) Am J Hum Genet 60: 842-850

SCA3:
5. Kawaguchi, Y. et al. (1994) Nature Genetics 8: 221-228
6. Maciel, P. et al. (1995) Am J Hum Genet 57: 54-61

SCA6:
7. Zhuchenko, O. et al. (1997) Nature Genetics 15: 62-69

SCA7:
8. Koob, M.D. et al. (1998) Nature Genetics 18: 72-75
9. David, G. et al. (1997) Nature Genetics 17: 65-70
10. Gouw, L.G. et al. (1998) Hum Mol Genet 7: 525-532
11. Johansson, J. et al. (1998) Hum Mol Genet 7: 171-176

SCA8:
12. Koob, M.D., et al. (1999) Nature Genetics 21: 379 -384
13. Moseley, M.L . et al. (1998) Am J Hum Genet 63(4; suppl.) P. A336, Abst. 1944

SCA10:
14. Matsuura, T., et al. (2000) Nature Genetics 26: 191-194

SCA17:
15. Fujigasaki, H., et al (2001) Brain 124: 1939 -1947
16. Nakamura, K., et al (2001) Hum Mol Genet 10: 1441 - 1448
17. Zuhlke, C., et al (2001) Eur J Hum Genet 9: 160 - 164

DRPLA:
18. Koide, R. et al. 1994. Nature Genet. 6: 9-13
19. Nagafuchi, S. et al. 1994. Nature Genet. 6: 14-17

SCA14 (PRKCG):
20. Chen, D.-H. et al. (2003) Am J Hum Genet 72: 839-849
21. Yabe, I. et al. (2003) Arch Neurol 60: 1749-1751
22. van de Warrenburg, B. et al. (2003) Neurology 61: 1760-1765

SCA5 (*SPTBN2*):
23. Ikeda, Y., et al., Nature Genetics (2006) 38: 184-190.

GLOSSARY

DNA variants are deviations from a gene's reference sequence. In recessive diseases, mutations must be found in both alleles of the a gene to confirm the presence of the disease. In dominant diseases, only a single mutation in the gene is necessary to confirm the presence of the disease. Disease-causing mutations can be homozygous or compound heterozygous. It is not uncommon to have more than two types of DNA sequence variants detected in a gene. In addition, the clinical significance of individual variant types and their combinations differs widely. The DNA variant types and additional terminology utilized in the report are

Diagnosis Service Rep

Patient	Requesting Physician	Accession Number 06017750
Social Security Number	Report to	Family Number/Kindred Number
Specimen Type Whole Blood	Address	Patient Number 999529
Test Category Not Available	Pathology Department	Specimen Collection Date 04/03/2006
Test Requested Dominant Ataxia Evaluation		Accession Date 04/05/2006
	Additional Reports to:	Report Date 06/06/2006

explained below. (Consult the Technical Results and Comments section of this report to determine if any of the following apply to this individual.)

DNA Variant or Result Types:

1. Known disease-associated mutations are documented in the literature to be associated with disease. In a recessive disease, an affected individual can be homozygous for such a mutation (the same recessive mutation present on both chromosomes) or a compound heterozygote (with different recessive mutations present on each chromosome), while an unaffected carrier has a single mutation on one chromosome. In a dominant disease, an affected individual typically has a single mutation on one chromosome.

2. Predicted disease-associated mutations are expected to result in significant alteration of the structure and function of the protein encoded by the gene. Typical examples include frame shift mutations, splicing mutations, nonsense mutations, and deletions or duplications of entire exons. In some cases, novel missense mutations are predicted to cause disease due to the extreme conservation and known function of the amino acid that is predicted to change. Current literature indicates that DNA sequence variants of these types are associated with disease. However, due to the absence of established genotype-phenotype correlations for this specific DNA sequence variant, this result should be carefully reconciled with this individual's clinical and family history.

3. Predicted amino acid changes of unknown significance are DNA sequence variants that are detected reproducibly, but have not been correlated with clinical presentation and/or pathology in the current literature, nor do they result in a readily predictable effect upon protein structure and function. The amino acid change is predicted based on simple interpretations of the genetic code. However, these same types of alterations may sometimes alter normal gene splicing and processing, and thereby cause more significant and unpredictable effects. Since these types of sequence variants are similar to those observed in disease-associated mutations and benign polymorphisms, the nature of this variation prohibits definitive interpretation.

4. Variants of unknown clinical significance are DNA sequence variants that are detected reproducibly, but have not been correlated with clinical presentation and/or pathology in the current literature, nor do they result in a readily predictable effect upon protein structure and function. Typical examples include single nucleotide changes in the coding or non-coding regions of the gene that are sometimes labeled as "silent mutations", or "intronic polymorphisms." These types of alterations often have no effect, but may sometimes alter normal gene splicing and processing. Since these types of sequence variants are similar to those observed in disease-associated mutations and benign polymorphisms, the nature of this variation prohibits definitive interpretation.

5. Inconclusive test results are those unable to be interpreted as either

Diagnosis Service Re

Patient	Requesting Physician	Accession Number 06017750
Sex F / Social Security Number	Report to	Family Number/Kindred Number
Specimen Type Whole Blood	Address	Patient Number 999529
Test Category Not Available	Pathology Department	Specimen Collection Date 04/03/2006
Test Requested Dominant Ataxia Evaluation		Accession Date 04/05/2006
	Additional Reports to:	Report Date 06/06/2006

negative or positive due to a technical problem in the assay, and thus can rule out neither the presence nor absence of abnormalities in these genes. Inconclusive results are typically resolved by analysis of a repeat specimen. There will be no charge for the repeat analysis. Please indicate "REPEAT SPECIMEN" along with the above Athena Accession Number on the requisition. If a positive results was obtained for another gene analyzed in this profile, the submission of a repeat specimen may not be warranted.

6. Indeterminate test results, while methodologically accurate, are not clinically meaningful due to the lack of published clinical studies correlating test results in this specific category with clinical presentation and/or pathology. Due to the lack of published findings, these test results cannot be interpreted as either normal or abnormal. Indeterminate results are generally caused by test results that fall outside of the established interpretive criteria. Indeterminate test results are not resolved by analysis of a repeat specimen.

7. Benign polymorphisms are DNA sequence variants that have been documented in the literature to occur in the general unaffected population and have not been associated with disease, or those that are unpublished, but have been detected in Athena studies at a frequency of 2% or greater in a non-ataxia population.

****** FINAL REPORT ****** ver 1.0

This test was developed and its performance characteristics determined by Athena Diagnostics, Inc. has not been cleared or approved by the U.S. Food and Drug Administration. The FDA has determine that such clearance or approval is not necessary. This test is used for clinical purposes and should no regarded as investigational or for research only. Athena Diagnostics is licensed under the Clinic Laboratory Improvement Amendments of 1988 (CLIA) to perform high complexity clinical testing. Athena Diagnostics has performed assay validation studies and has developed its laborator protocols and operating procedures in consultation with experts in the field and in accordance with th standards of the National Committee on Clinical Laboratory Standards (NCCLS).

Laboratory results and submitted clinical information reviewed by,

Sat Dev Batish, PhD, FACMG
Chief Director, Genetics

William K Seltzer, PhD, ABMG
Director, Genetics

Narasimhan Nagan, PhD, ABMG
Director, Genetics

Laboratory oversight provided by Joseph J. Higgins, M.D., F.A.A.N., CLIA license holder, Athena Diagnostics (CLIA # 22D0069726)

Testing performed at:
Athena Diagnostics Four Biotech Park 377 Plantation St Worcester MA 01605

My Birth

I was born November 14, 1956 to my parent and my father who I thought was my father for years. I was a premature child at birth, I only weight 4 lbs. So back in the 50's if you were not a certain birth weight you had to stay in the hospital until you picked up weight. I stay in the hospital for 1 month before I could go home. My weight was 5 lbs I believe it was. My last name that I was born with is Queen. My father went home to be with the Lord in 1996. I am the product of a love affair or a one night stand that happened in the 1950's I do not know how long the relationship lasted. I have never been told the truth about my real father.

As I am growing up I notice my hair is red and my skin is lighter than my other siblings are. I keep going on with life not thinking about nothing at all, life is good. I am blessed child that was born to a man and a women who were married to different people at that time. I did not know this until I was a grown adult women and had 2 sons of my own.

My health was not as good as it should have been, I was anemic a lot and had to get glasses to see how to do my school work. I was a quite little girl who did talk much at all. I would get blame for things that were not done or they said I did. This was how it was for me, in this family, I went with the flow of things think everything is okay. Running to school because the dogs would chase after you if you just walk to school. Riding my bike around town in the small community that we lived in, enjoy, what I thought was my real life, as a Queen girl. I grew up at 8 years old work in the field picking cotton with a shack pulling on my back, picking berries, working in the field picking grapes as a young child had to work very hard, and not very focus on school work. Felt out of place and not encourage as a child dealing with all these things that happen to me. Was put into a special education class in elementary and tested out of in High School. Graduated in 3 ½ years from High School, and working on College as we speak, life as a way of working it self out. I was still working in the field after school and enjoy music, choir, and band at school time. I got to do some things, and a lot of things that I didn't like at all. Gods way of teaching you that you cant always get your way in life. There was favoritism in this family, put it all was a life lesson for me not to treat my sons that way I was treated in this family unit. You have to work hard in this life, nothing is free. I may have given my sons things that they did not need. or wanted to spoil them a little, but who does not want to give your child, what you did not have as a kid. I want my sons to work and do better than me. Find their own way. I know they will make mistakes along the way but God is able to carry them through all things that they have to go through. My sons did not have to go through all the things I went through to make money, the child safety laws protect the children now. You don't see a 8 year old out working in the field picking grapes, or cotton. They have to be in school and the law would be all over the parents for making children work out in the field. In school getting there education, and making sure the kids a plenty of rest at night. As a parent now there are laws against children working that young. That would be consider abuse of children, the parents would end up in trouble with the law. They would probably loss their children over working them in the fields like they did us. In the morning go work until lunch, eat lunch and go back to work until it was getting dark outside. When school started we work after school, and work until the sun would go down. It was hard trying to do school work, after dark, and tired, and had no food, in the house sometimes. But we made it through it all with a lot of extra help from teacher, and the school helping us to get through all of it. Being in a special education class to help me with my learning skills that I had problems with until I was in high school testes out of special aide in my sophomore year in high school. If you have a problem get help, I could not focus on school work and working after school. All the income burden that was put on the children at a early age, did not help me get my school work done, and not be behind in our study's. I wanted to be able to be a kid and have some fun, I had some fun it was with band and music, and choir and trips with the band was my escape from how my life really was.

My marriages

My first marriage when I was a young lady and in love. I thought as life went on, things happened and we were not together as a couple, we were just going through the motions of marriage.

We had two beautiful wonderful sons out of this marriage. 16 years of experience to learn how to treat the next spouse, that come into my life the next time. I was married to him in 1980's until 1996-1997 it ended in Divorce. My next marriage started in 2003 and was a shake one, with us moving to find work for my ex-husband to San Diego California. My family member is working in San Diego, and I start getting sick in La Mesa California. I end up at Hospital thinking I had a Stroke, because my right side of my face is dropping and my head is hurting. I had the MRI and not stroke, full ataxia in 2006. I was diagnosed with SCA5 Ataxia or Lincolns Ataxia. There was a lot of people that were in our lives for food, shelter, and money. They would steal from our home. I was tired of having all these people coming into our home without respect of personal things. There was a door bell put on the door, so we could here when the door was open, and know who was in the house. Looking back this was not a marriage this was just for shelter. My family member was never at home with me always had to go, and leave again right after he got in the house. He was never where he said he would be, We were married for 7 years, I could not drive myself because of my ataxia, so he would take me to pay bills or get food, and then go and leave me sitting at home alone. He would be gone for hours on end, before it was late he come in. He would say I am help this person or that person. This marriage ended in 2011. I was tried of being left alone all the time. As of 2011 to 2015 I am a single christian women of God, working to improve herself in all that she does to glorify the father in heaven. I had no peace are joy in this relationship because I would see my family member leave and then come back and leave again claiming he had to do something for someone else. I would walk around my home wondering what he was doing. I could not take this anymore I had to end this marriage of lies and deceit. While in this marriage I was always using walls, chairs, walkers to keep me from falling down. When using the shower I had a shower chair for 5 to 6 years. I did not drive a car because of riding in one made my head spin around and felt dizziness. I had to close my eyes and not look at the road because I would get so lite head, and off balance from just riding in the car. For a long time I was not able to look at the road while someone else was driving.

In my first marriage I had to go to driving school to get a drivers license to drive a car, I was so embarrassed by not having a drivers license to drive a car. No one showed me at home, or had the time to teach me how to drive a car. Every one who got there license were given time and patient to do it

All they wanted was money. I pass my driving school and got my drivers License in southern California, I was so happy to final have my drivers license.

My Life Story

My home life was very uncomfortable because I was not a talker, like I am now. I felt I had no voice to speak for myself, or I was very afraid to talk for myself. Some of my siblings would pick on me, because I did not talk for a good reason, just looking at how they treated me, or what they wanted from me in the future. It went on for a long time not talking in elementary, and Junior High, and High School. Until I got so tired of it and explode on my family about my school clothes, family member would get into my closet and take my clothes and wear it, and it never came back the same way it left. So I chased family member around this big brown ugly house. Maybe four or five times until she got tired, and ran upstairs and lock the door in her room. This sibling was always wearing my shoes, dress, anything that she though she could wear. I was upset, mad, angry, with this family member. I had enough and started speaking up for myself. I was angry with the parent who did not do any thing to stop all the drama that was going on in the home.

We had to work hard to keep food on the table, and support our parent and boyfriend. I feel they decide to make us work, to make lives easier for the parent so the parent would get hurt by the boyfriend. This went on for years, and the family grew worse because of lack of unity, a large division was in this family. I always wanted to stay away from home, and be with my friends.

this story is about a lie that has been going on since my birth in 1956. The was about who my father was It has final ended at age 50 years old when I was diagnosed with Ataxia 5 2006. The father who I though was my father is not my biological father. He told me in his California home the same year of my Ataxia 5 diagnosed from my Neurologist in San Diego California. He is listed on the birth certificate as the father of me. He may not of been in town for my birth, or even around. In my heart I am speechless and could not talk, and went and check in to a hotel to hide from all of this with my family member. I cry for days, and felt like I was not worth the family being honesty, who deceived me and hide the truth. The main parent should of told me the truth, the main parent responsibility to do the right thing, and let me know what is the truth. This disease can effect my two sons that I had. I have felt that everyone lied and cover it up for such a long time. I move back to the small town that I am from recently in 2007, I feel my marriage is getting worst and not better, because his wife of 14 years starts coming around and wants him to care for her also, so that not a good sign at all. Still had no clue who my father was. Until my family member told me also about what my parent said about my father. So I started looking on ancestry. com for answers, and got my first leaf from that site. My father was born 10 May 1918 passed away November 15, 1996. Never got to meet him, but felt like someone was watching over me from a far. My parent would go get food from his restaurant that he own at that time and I enjoyed the food that was served from his business. Only I did not know he was my father at that time. I called my father business, his ex wife answer the phone and said she would get back to me. It took few weeks for her to get back to me. She called back and he knows about you and wants nothing to do with you, and leave us alone and don't call again contact us again. So that was they end of that, journey 2009 of connecting with my family member.

What is done in the dark in the shall come to the light. Thank God I got my answer Unfortunate I could not have a family member or father relationship with either of them. But God has a plan for my life, when one door closes they other door opens for you. I have always tried to be positive about life and what lesson I have to learn, while I am in the storm of life, for forgiveness is a big part of it. The lesson may be hard to deal with at first, put have to go through the fire, to polish you and mole you into this wonderful child of God who forgives and moves on with life. Why forgive, because it you don't forgive, you will care it in your heart, for ever and never let it go. That person who done you wrong is living life not thinking about your feeling, or what has happened. For me it is a work in progress working on forgiveness. Writing this book will help me with how I feel about the whole thing as I keep going on with it. I will have feeling of angry and pain, and lies from all this put I will come out of it a better person, with a good heart towards all who decided not to tell the truth for a long time. I will not hide under a rock for all of these lies, and untruths that have been going on for years of my life. It time to put my voice on paper, and not be silent and write what is on my heart that I want to say about my treatment. On this issue of my father, he existent on this earth he had right to be in my life if he wanted to, it was his choice to make. My parents were married to other people so that made it hard for them, living in the 50's and 60's and70's 80's having a half white and half black child was a secret they had to keep from me for years. I am the love child from that one night stand or love affair, that happened many years ago, it funny I think that way, no one has ever told me anything about it, If I was a plan birth or a mistake. I choose to think, I am a blessed child, and keep going with my life. I finish high School in 1975 and took some college classes, like music a lot, played in the high school band and the school choir.

My older sibling and I had to become they adults in the home, because the situation calls for us to step up and work and make money to pay for food, shelter, gas and electricity, because the boyfriend was put his hands on the parent in the home. Some of us that did not have to work just enjoy the fruits of others labor. This went on for years of my life working and trying to finish high school as a child in this family God had to give me the strength to make it to the next day.

. It had got so bad the children were asking us for money for their personal needs to take care of, for example shoe, clothing, books, lunch money. All ways with hands out, but we had no one to put our hands out when we need it. It was like we were trying to go forward, and ended 10 steps back in the same spot over and over again. We could never save our money for what we wanted, like a new pair of shoes, pants that someone went and put on and stretch out your only pair. This was cycle that was never going to stop, It felt as if they were taking the life out of me in this home. My soul wanted to be free of all this and hurry up and graduated from high school. Leave all this pain behind me for ever, and not think about it again. I had to learn how to be myself and work for me and not give everything I made away, I was so use to giving it all away, and not having anything for myself. I was so free in my spirit from just leaving this place, that cause me so much pain. I am happy and want to do great things for my family and friends that I love. I like doing crafts, like knitting scarfs and making art projects with my grandchildren. I have 7 grandchildren that are a wonderful blessing to me, that like to share their ideas and dreams of greatness for themselves. I want to tell them all things are possible in their dreams, if you can dream it you can be it. Look at me I am writing a book. I have always dreamed of writing a book, but never thought I could do it. I hope to inspire everyone who has a dream or a passion to go for it and not give up on it, finish the race that is in front of us. Give God the glory for all of it, without him moving in our lives, we could not move or make things happened for ourselves. Keep moving towards Gods best for yourself. I have learn to share my time wisely, not over booking myself, Keep my charity work two or three things I can handle, and do what is in your heart to do.

My Hospital stay

I walked into Hospital on my own power. I was able to speak and talk, but after a couple of hours sitting in the emergency room waiting to see the doctor on call their. They exam me and checked me for a stroke, My face is drooping on my right side of my face and a headache in my head. I was put into the hospital for observation for symptoms that I had. I was put into a room by myself observation, my signs were muscle spams in my feet, so they put padding around my bed for my protection so would hurt myself. I received a sandwich to eat before I went to be for the night, watch television before I tried to sleep. I had a big day the next day, MRI in the morning, the Numerologist comes in and puts me through test balance test and coordination test and then put a gait belt around me and walking me down the hall and keeps me from falling down. He orders the following a walker and a blood test all this is to be done before I go home that evening. The MRI is done that same day, I was given a pill to relax me before I go into the machine so the can check if I had a stroke. The MRI showed no stroke, full ataxia, not a stroke. I remember being in the tube lie there looking at the inside of the machine thin king what is going on with me. I was not scared just did not know what was wrong with me. You could here the machine going and do one was talking, just looking at the images of my head. I felt like I was on display in this machine.

I was released to go home at eleven o'clock that night. Went into wheel chair out of hospital and into our car home with my stuff and medication for high blood pressure pills, cholesterol pills and a walker that I was to use to get around. I went in one way and come out with a walker that I had to use to get around in my home or shopping. Started to go to this clinic to get help with medications and blood pressure pills. 2 months later went to my neurologist and he told my test results from my blood work. He ask me if I knew any one in Abraham Lincoln's family, My family member and I had a puzzled look on our face. I was shocked at what this neurologist was saying to me about if I knew Abraham Lincoln's family. I had no clue about his family or any thing that was saying, I was apart of his world. I know of him in books, that I have see and that was it.

It all made sense to me now, all the name calling that had been said, when I was a young girl about my color, and me not understanding why this person was calling me that mean word. My father was a white man not a black man like I thought. This was a shock to my system, and a surprise that I was not expecting to come out. Of the doctors mouth. I had the task of finding the truth for myself and uncovering my truth, of my life.

Speech and Physical therapy

I started speech and physical therapy, when I had my last visit with my Neurologist he notice my voice was different and my words were slurred together. I was riding in at hospital van to go to all these appointments that I had, 3 times a week speech and 2 times a week physical therapy, after I got of the hospital 2006. I did balance and gait training I saw a Neurologist in Fresno California and ask if I could be put in Physical therapy in 2014. I wanted to work on my balance and coordination, gait and walk better, this make sure I not have any falls, by using these exercise I feel much better. Using a stationary bike for strength and different stretches as my exercise program went I had to do bridges, balance board, close my eyes with my feet normal width apart, balance on one leg, and walking on grass because it felt different on grass. I did this therapy because I walk a lot, my feet were wide when I walked, because of my balance was not right. My feet are together not wide apart as they were when I started in the therapy program. I worked at for 2 or 3 months in therapy with a gate belt around my waist, walking stepping over high and low things that they put in front of me to step over. This is my program for the rest of my life. It is good for me to do this for myself so I would not have any falls in the future, and continue to move, and learn new things. I am always will to learn new things and use my creative ideas to better myself and my family for the future generation to come. I love life and talking to positive people who inspire you to dream and encourage you to go for it. My family member told me to go for it and dream big. This is my story of my life and my pain and sorrow of all my life.

My dreams is to write a book, I am fulling my dream of writing a book about my life, health, ataxia 5, music, high school, parent, family members, sons grandchildren, what I have learned about me, doing the writing process, that forgiveness is free, so you can move on in life. Having sad moments and learning to forgive is hard to do. You can say you forgive and carry it in your heart, and not really forgive that person for what they have done. Until you make up in your mind to really for give that person for making you feel like your not that valued to them. I had good times in life as well as the bad times, that come alone The bad out weight the good times, in most of my childhood memory's I was not talking or being told on that I did something, when I know I did not do anything at all, and getting in trouble, and the family member telling the lie laughing at me. I get sent to my room with out eating dinner. That was not fun for me to be apart of as a child. Another example was having to use a school instrument for band, and the family member getting her instrument purchase for them. Or marching in a parade and your parent would tell the band teacher to pull you out before the competition starts. I would be walking on the side as if you were not good enough to be in competition. They other sibling would be marching in the parade through the competition. If I was doing that bad why did they help me to become better in my marching? My other sibling could of worked with me it I was having problems, if that was the case. I could of done better with help, and practice marching, I did practicing marching at the school on the streets with the band on weekends and during school, I feel I was good enough to be out there to march. Put life goes on and I will make it to the beautiful country, and enjoy all it has to offer without, having a band instrument or uniform on to enjoy all it has to offer. I will be happy to see all of it. Life is too short to worry about all that stuff like that in the first place.

It will be my time to see it and be apart of it one day soon. This has been a dream of my to go and see it for along time.

My health now

My health is a lot better know I am able to walk without a walker or wheel chair. With God's help and the help of many medical professional. I have come along way, and plan to go further with God's help. My son told me not to use the walker, in 2011 when I was going through my divorce and the death of my other father. My son told me mom you don't need the walker you can walk without it that was the most scariest that I had to try to do by myself, this was a hard task for me. I was walking with my feet far apart from each other, because I did not want to fall down. I have more training now so it is more easier for me to walk, without stressing over if, I am going to fall on my face. I can take my grandchildren to the park and play with out having a walker, and enjoy it much better. I Love walking around, window shopping, just seeing all the beautiful flowers, and the trees that has been provided for us to enjoy, on this earth. I feel much better my clothes fit better, and I sleep and rest at night, and do my work that I need to get done.

When I walk I feel the air on my face and walking helps me release the stress of that day. The air blowing in my face, and my feet moving fast down the street. To me that is a blessing from God for me to be dong that 6 years ago I couldn't not move like that. I have high blood pressure that is under control from walking and doing exercise. My cholesterol is under control also, by watching what I eat and taking medications. And exercise has help my over all health to improve a lot.

My Mother's Day 2014

I was pick up in my son's and he open the door for me, I didn't know what was in store for me. With their I pads and phones we were off to the restaurant for my Mothers Day brunch. There was no one in the seat of the van, I know I looked We are almost there and Michel Jackson is playing on the stereo in the van. That is my favorite music that I listen to when I was growing up in the 70's. I am enjoying the music and happy, and the camera are rolling and I pad is going, they stop the car and park away from the restaurant. The special clue is said happy mother day, and out pops my other son that was in the back of the van in the storage area with red roses and a Mother's Day card, I was surprised and shocked he scared me because I thought I was alone in the van. I had not seen my other son on mothers day for a very long time. It was a blessing to see both of them at the same time to come and celebrate me for mothers day. My mothers day was put on YouTube for the world to see. I am dancing away not thinking about any one is in the back of the van and there he comes with my flowers and a card. Had a great breakfast and was truly blessed by that experience that I had with my son's, and they have made me a very proud mother. I love both of them with all my heart and my soul. This shows me that God has touch them and made his face shine on both of them. I want nothing put the best for both of my young adult sons. I want God to bless them and keep them this is my prayer for them. I remember when they were young and playing out in the yard, and playing ball and chasing each other around the yard. Feeding the sheep they raise for the fair, and all that getting ready for fair. My most valued memory was when both of them were born, and graduated from high school, that is the most precious life experience for me. When my first grandchild was born, I was so excited to be a grandmother for the first time, I was jumping up and down like a kid in a candy store. This was a great day in my life. I final had life lessons to pass on to my grandchildren, and show them how to do things, and play, with them inside, or outside, and not get in trouble with their parents. All these experience I will always cherish them as a blessing that God has given me. I was able to walk into my mother's Day lunch on my own and enjoy, the food that I had. It was a blessed day.

My 58th Birthday

On my 58th birthday I was called and told to get ready for breakfast at Denny's Restaurant for my birthday had a wonderful breakfast with my son and daughter in law and new grandson. Enjoyed the evening later with my family coming and bring pizza and cupcakes and gift that brought for me. This was a blessed night for me. I enjoyed my birthday month very much. Had a great time with my grandchildren and my son and his wife that evening. Many of my birthdays I have had a wonderful time with my family. They usually take me to dinner for my birthdays, and the workers would bring me a desert and sing happy birthday to me. All my birthdays were happy for me, and I enjoyed them. I expect to have a wonderful 59th birthday if God is will and able for me to see that day.

My long time friend

I have a long time friend from school about 30 years or so. We were very close at one time in our lives, I have been very busy in my life, I think about her often. We went to high school activities, football games, in college. We shared things in each other lives, and how we could learning more and be more positive in all things. I have lost touch with her put she is in my prayer, because she is a breast cancer survivor. We have been sisters forever in past years we have lost touch.

We have talked I think last year on visiting each other, My lack of transportation to get around hinders things some times. I wish her well with all the things that she is doing for herself and her family. We would ride the van together to college, and eat lunch and breakfast together, hide from my family member who want money all the time. The place were would go to would be the college library, to study for our classes. We spent time at her home when we were young,

Learning again

Learning to keep your balance is a very hard thing to do. I have to work at it for the rest of my life, as long as I am still living on this earth. If feels different learning to keep your balance as adult you have done it before it not new. It your way keeping yourself together, and well for the time that you have left on this earth. As a child it is fresh and new and exciting for the parent to see the child walking and moving around without problems. For adult it is about getting around and being able to take care of myself and being able to function with your disability on your own power, and your own terms. Excepting your limitation and moving on with life, is all that a person can do in this life.

Making mistakes and learning from them and living life to it fullest. The whole thing changed for the better. I became aware of who I really was, I could teach my children and my grandchildren to love and be honest and work hard, and have love in their hearts, and compassion for his or her fellow man in need of food or shelter.

My Parent

My parent did the best that they could with all the things that were going on in their lives. Both of them had separate lives with their boyfriend or wife. I feel like it could of being different with the choice of who they wanted to be with. It was there choice to make, I had no say in who they dated or married. I will say I do forgive and excepted what has happen in my life, And wish all of them the best that God has to offer them. I must continue in my life journey to better myself by learning and doing Gods word. I do not hate you, I was angry with you for a long time for not tell the truth of who my real father was. as a child and all the lies that was cover up by other people to keep your secret safe for 50 years of my life. May God bless you and keep you is my prayer for you this day. This is my way of healing myself of all the pain that was cause to me. In my early years of life. When I did speak I could not get the words out fast enough for fear they would not let me speak at all. That is why I would raise my voice in anger over things. I felt I was not heard, at all if I said something when I was a child. I am a work in progress, and please pray for me to finish my race that is in front of me. To be a help and a blessing to some one who may need it today. I know I am not they only one in this world this has happened to. I hope to learn from this experience and to forgive and move on with life.

Nothing was wasted

In my journey none of my experiences was wasted. All the things that I had to go through in my life. My birth, I have made improvement in my health nothing was wasted. My life as a child, that did not talk much, nothing was wasted. Know I talk a lot nothing was wasted. The lies I had to live with nothing was wasted Now I know the truth, so nothing was wasted. The fathers who I found to be my fathers nothing was wasted. God is giving me a voice to speak up about all that has happened in my life. I will see both of my parent in heaven so nothing was wasted. Family miss treatment had to happen. It help me to speak up say I am tired of how I have been treated all those years. so nothing was wasted. My relationships ending, made me look at myself, start speaking up and telling my future husband what I expect out of my future relationships to become a better person nothing was wasted in my life experiences. Everything that I went through was to prepare me for life and pass the test. Nothing that I have went through in my life was wasted, I have learned from it either not to do it anymore or to continue and persevere in it until the end of time. We all have that light bulb moment in time when we figure out what our mistakes are, and try to correct it, and go another direction. That voice inside you telling you this is not the right think to do. It the inner man speaking out and saying look at what you are doing, you should pay attention. Ask God for guidance in any matter that you have to go through, that is what I would do. I know not everyone is a God person that is okay, but one day you will call on him, and every knee shall bend, and every tongue shall confess, that Jesus is Lord. When you get ready to leave this earth, you set your affairs in order with people, and family, and God. If you live with good intention for others nothing will be wasted, because you get it back from other people you help along the way. This how I live with good intention towards other nothing is wasted from my life. Just blessing will flow in my life. I have meany blessing to be thankful for having a forgiving heart and will to help other that are in need of things in life. For being a quite and kind person, and want to help others, I have wonderful sons, and grandchildren, my one parent is still living that is a blessing. This book is to help me heal my heart, of all the pain that I had to live with all my life By put this book out in a positive let reader know even people, who are not famous have trials and pains in life. I have seen many things and lived to the best of my ability as a ordinary person who has many trail in life but God has gotten me through it.

My experiences

My experience growing up in the 50's I was born, but not much segregation in the state I lived in. There was a lot of segregation, when we travel to Arkansas to visit family in the 60's. It was very different the had white's bathrooms and blacks bathrooms, whites drinking fountains, and colored water fountains only and White Restaurants. If you wanted food you had to go to the back of the restaurant to get food. When we traveled we had our water and food to eat because of the way things were in the South. I saw a large group of high school boys walking home after practicing football. They were African American in full gear dirty need showers, they could not use the same bathroom as the the white football players. Where I am from there was no segregation at all, but in the south there was people not able to ride a public bus to the store in the front seat of the bus, They had to ride in the back of the bus. Thank God For Dr Martian Luther King If he did not stand up for us, we would probably still be in segregation worse then we are now. It not as bad as it was back, then, it still exist in some small rural areas, with there mine set on the way it was back then. We have seen many President from the 50's and 60's and 70's and 80's. I was born in 1956 the 34th President was Dwight D Eisenhower, was in office from January 20,1953 to January 20, 1961. I don't remember any thing about that this President at all. I was only 5 years old when he left office and had no interest in that kind of stuff, just playing with my dolls. The 35th President was John F. Kennedy he was in office from January 20,

1961 to November 22, 1963 when he was assassinated. Everyone who watched was sadden about his assassinated. I remember watching on a black and white TV at school and though this was a good President, was sad because he seem like he really care about the people, he was trying to help. The 36th president that took office was was Lyndon B Johnson he was in office November 22,1963 and was sword in office on an airplane. The news was talking about him being sword while flying back to the White House. R elected fora a second term until January 20, 1969, I know nothing about this president. The one I heard a lot about was the 37th President which was the fourth President of the 60's was Richard Nixon. This President office in January 20, 1969 until August 9, 1974. I know of him because of the news talking about the Watergate scandal, forcing him to resign his office. This was very bad for the government, the people were outraged with this event that happened in the 60's. President Ford took office after the Watergate scandal. He gave Nixon a pardon. President Ford was not reelected for a second term probably because of the pardon. My thinking on this when I was a college student there not suppose to be spying on other people in the first place. President Jimmy Carter was a peanut farmer, that is all I know about him. He was our 39th President. The 40th President was Ronald Reagan 1981 to 1989. President Reagan is credited with reviving national pride after the turmoil of the 60's, and 70's, he was a popular President and they only President to survive after being wounded by a would-be assassin. I remember watch this at my home with my sons. I though this was very hard to watch the President was shout, and rush to the hospital, and the secret service was covering him securing the area. God has blessed me to see and hear all these things that have happened in the United States of America. I like riding bikes, reading books, running track I did not get to do much of because I had to work after school. I was quite as child, and did not speak much at all. My friends spoke for me or help me fight my battles in school. This carry to my home life I was picked on at home. I had no where to feel safe from being picked on. I remember walking upstairs and one of my siblings threw a cat on my back and scratched my back. This was in the summer time with short sleeves on, there was a time when I think decided not to talk because my voice was not going to be heard in this dysfunctional family that I was in. I did not communication with my family at that time because they were using their power to do what they wanted all the time. They did not care about your feelings at all. It was about them all the time, they knew it, and they love to make us feel like we were not of value at all. That is what I though as a child growing up with them.

Music I Liked

The music I like when I was growing up in the 50's and 60's and 70's the beetles, earth wind and fire, Steve Wonder, Marvin G aye, Smokey Robinson, Donna Summer, Jackson 5, Tina Turner, Diane Ross and the supreme, Al Green, Prince in purple rain, We would play records on the record player and dance on the porch in the house after our chore were done, on Saturdays and watch soul train and American Band Stand in the afternoon. This was our fun time after chores were done. I like a lot of gospel music Byron Cage, Kirk Franklin, Mary Mary, Dorinda Clark Cole, Colorado mass Choir, Martha Munizzi, J Moss, This is what I listen to now, Bruno Mars, songs when I was young I like the Beatles, rolling stones, they were fun to watch on the black in white television.

Dancing

I like dancing at the dances it help me forget about how like was not kind, to this child. It was fun to dance with friends in a group and not have to have a boyfriend. Music for me was a way of easy the pain of life. I could tune out all the bad that happened to me that day. I went to church with my family and thought the church we were going to was a real church. The people would were over it were running it like a club. Collect dues and put the money in their pocket, none of it went to the bank. They were robbing God. I learn this when I was an adult and decided to attend another church. My church experience was my parent played the piano, and sang, and the boyfriend was a deacon in the church. This is hard to explain, I always thought that they were married, that why all the problems happen in that family because they were not married to each other or committed to one another. My parent had a fake marriage license on the wall for us to see that they were married. Everything about this family was not real. I live in a fake home. with fake people until I moved out of the home

Speaking

It took me a long time to start talking, and when I did I exploded on people with a bang. I thought if I don;t get out they are going to stop me from saying what I had to say. I was always blamed for things in that fake house that I call my home. Until I explored on people who would say things that were not true about what I did or did not do. It is important to be able to speak up for yourself. But I was doing it the wrong way. I had to learn with Gods help to be softer and kinder with my words.

It hard to change from a non speaker to a speaker, you have to work on listen and talking to the person, and I was use to being alone and not being bother by anyone. I was tried of the family thinking that they could do or say anything and I was not gong to do anything about it.

So I started to talk to them and speak up for myself. I was so tried of all of the bull that was going on in the home. Blaming the workers for the stuff that was not done so the Princess could sit and do nothing all day. I felt like Cinderella who could not go to the ball, because she was not good enough for the family functions.

Even Cinderella got her happy ending in that story. My speaking for myself was one of my victory in my life. Because I was afraid to say anything at all for along time. I always felt intimidated by family, not knowing it they care about me as a family member. It just hit me like a ton of bricks, no one ever told me that they loved me in that home at all. That why I never talked that much in the family, as a child. My sibling would get spanking, because they would talk back to the parent. I did not speak up for myself, I would get sent to my room up stairs with out dinner, because of a lie that was told on me.

What a wake up call for me to realize that now at my age of 58 years old, I don't remember my parent saying those words to me at all. I have worked hard got in trouble, for not rolling trays fast enough and cut grapes and, was stung by a wasp, and had to go home, ended up at the hospital because I was a;allergic to bees and wasps. I was given a shot and sent home, so the swelling would go down. I do not remember how many days I stay home, but I did have to go back out their to work in the fields. again. They other siblings did not have to work hard, they went out there and was putting a paper tray down on the ground, had the ring in her hand and feel back straight on the ground. And never had to go back out there again to work in the field. That was how it was in that family, the parent would say you don't have a father. And you cant do this or that. I remember lining up to give my check to the parent so they could go cash it and spend on what ever they wanted, I guess because the shelves were bare, no food in the refrigerator, lights got turn off, and the rent was not payed. I learn that in the 89-90 that they were going to Foreclose on for 7,000 dollars. They were calling around for money to save the house. The end up losing the home and had to move to a one bed room apartment,

My Sons

My sons are 4 years apart form each other. They are hard working adult men, I had my hands full when they were young, loved sports, games football, cars girls, phone all the thing teenagers like to do. I was co parenting with my ex-husband, it was a challenge to raise two high energy boys. Always building things, riding animals around our property, jumping off haystacks, chasing each other around the property. Both of my sons played basketball in high school. They enjoyed it. They always told me to not yell so loud at the games. I never listen to them about yelling at the game, I did what I wanted at the game if they did something great I cheer for them. I have had 4 pregnancy and only two of them made to this earth. They other 2 are up with God the father who knows all that I have went through.

I try to raise my boys to help others in the community that are in need of a helping hand. To be honesty in your dealings and treat others with respect, and love in their hearts.

We as parents do the best that we can with our children, while they are young, when they get older they do what they want to, and think they know it all. When they get out in the real word, they find it a hard and unkind place to be as a young adult. I pray I did the right things with my sons, and give them to God so he can be there for them and they talk to him. I wish them the best for both of my sons, and God keep them, and let God lead them in the right direction is my prayer for them. I am not perfect, but I did the best I could do with both of my sons. I learn to be soft in my speaking to them because. I yell at them a lot, when they were young. My sons did not understand, I did not talk a lot when I was their age, I was angry about my family life. I did not have a great family life. I did the best that I could do for them. It was hard raising sons, in the 1980 and 90's we work as a team to get through all of it. My sons have been there for me when I was really sick with my Ataxia 5. They seen me at my worst, lost of balance and coordination and all of the things that go with this inherited diseases of the nervous system. My son's have encourage me to keep on going, and let me know that I can do all things through Christ Jesus. Writing a book is one of the things that I want to do for myself, and learn a different language, knitting new things, and being more creative with my work, Being a role model for my son's and grandchildren. And to be a good citizen, honor your words, by doing what you say your going to do. Being friendly with others and sharing, what I think is important for my sons to know and pass it on to my grandchildren.

Family members

My Parent had 5 different fathers in the family that were married men. 4 girls and one boy, in boy friend Sanders, and one girl in the Greens, one girl in the Brown family, one girl in Smith family, and one in the Crouch family. My step brother and sisters that I have not seen in a long time. At this time in my life I just want to be left alone and live my life in peace and quiet, with no stress or drama from any of them. I want to see the world and enjoy the time I have on this beautiful earth that God has given all of us to enjoy. Live it to the fullest and and not have any regrets about how I lived my life of joy, and peace, and happiness, no family drama. I want peace and harmony in my life no drama at all. All my life there was drama and deceit, lies.. I want a honesty life, and not my passed life I love my family, put don't like the drama that they bring with them. I feel like everything that happened in my life was a lie. They took my life from me by not telling me, who my other family was. Allowing me to believe that this was my total family, passing this on all these years. Then I have to look at it as a blessing, this is allowing to speak for myself and show them that I have a forgiving heart. That wants to move on with life, and be blessed with my life and family.

All the sickness, and health issues, miss treatment by others, that I have live through in this family, has made me stronger, and I know my biological father would be proud of me. I feel I did it with grace and joy and love in my heart. Thinking this is my real life, I did not know any different. My heavenly father has help me to except all that has happened to me, and give me understanding of all of it.

So I can move forward in life with forgiveness in my heart for all who have wronged me in the pass. Forgiveness is for me, it frees your soul and your spirit man, from all that has happened in my life. This is for someone who is going through something worse than I have been through, I want all my readers to know you can have peace and joy when you forgive them and yourself for believing that everything was the truth and it was not the truth, for not knowing the signs of a lie that you have been living for 50 years of your life. I felt like I was not a valued person all my 50 years of my life, with people stringing me along with their lies. It like looking at a book and reading all the fairy tales you see in a book. This is not true story but a made up one, that is being told to me, as my life. I believed it for a long time, and now I feel like a fool with egg on my face. The truth shall set you free of all the lies that have been told to me all these years, and the tears I have cried over this father thing.

I am getting better with my life as time goes on. I am a work in progress and my God will get the victory over this, and the praise from it also. This is how you mess up a child with your lies and not being honesty with a child about their parents. If it good or bad the child needs to know the truth about where they came from, and not hold back the truth because the parents is scared or ashamed of what they have done in the past. We all are human and have made many mistakes in life, so just tell the truth and free yourself from the guilt that you hold on so tightly. We can not judge someone else mistakes, without looking at our own mistakes in life. I am not judging my parent for choosing not to tell me the truth. Everyone has to answer for themselves about what they did or did not do. My place is to get over it and move on with life, and find Gods best for myself, and pray for them to seek Gods forgiveness and keep it moving towards Gods best for themselves. Life is to short to hold on to the past pains of yesterday, and bring it to the present. We only have one life to live we should all live to to the fullest that we can, with out fear or pain of the past that we care inside of us. Talk to someone who will give you wisdom about things, in your life that you want to let go of and move on. Some one who will keep it confidential between you and that person. Parents need to stand up and tell the truth, I see so many court shows with women doing DNA testing because they were with so many men, they don't know who the father is. It simple answer to that is make better choices about your life. Be accountable for your actions, because there is a positive and a negative side to it. The truth will come out, it may not be today, but it will appear one day, what will you do then? If I would never gotten sick, like I did I would of never knew, of my father or my genealogy, of Josiah Lincoln. That was Gods way of telling me something is wrong in your life. It not what you think it is, look at this I here to comfort you, and walk you through this hard time, or trail that you will have to walk through, to get to the other side, and be happy. Thank God for giving me the skill and the knowledge to walk through it and make me a kind person with a loving heart for people. I could of turn out to be evil person with a lot of hate in my heart for my parent and family who keep it from for a long time in my life. That's not how I feel at all, I pray they have good health and blessing in there lives, and peace and joy may be with them. I was very angry with all of them but as time goes by, it not that important to me anymore. I just want to live on this earth with the power and grace to praise the Lord for all that he has done for me. I think if you praise your way through trials, you get to the other side of the problem and wonder how you got the victory. That is what I have been trying to do for myself praise him in all things good and bad. Keep God first in your life and you will go far in life

Second Father pass away

In 2011 on March 13, 2011 I remember this date because my father who I knew most of my life. Was living with me in our apartment he work up and knock on my door, He was on oxygen and a machine was on. I went to check on him and sad he was fine. I went to make his breakfast, I was in the kitchen cooking, his oatmeal for him, I listen for him to come out. He never came out of the bathroom. He had fell and pass away in the bathroom on that Sunday morning. I went in the bathroom and found him on the floor of the the bathroom. I ran to the phone and called 911 operator said check and see it he is breathing I could not find a pulse at all. The ambulance and the fire department came and they pronounce him dead at the scene. I cried, and cried over him a lot I want a father figure in my life My son came and I was still crying over him. I had bonded with him so much and my heart was breaking over his passing. My son came to comfort me, I had loss the only father figure I had knew for all these years. I got to spend his last 4 months with him, I know I did everything for him before he left this earth. He told me to stay away from my other family members, they did not come to see him in his last days. He want to see the other family members but they were in trouble with the law, or something like that, I did not know that at the time of his death. I called them to come and help me with cleaning up the floor of my apartment. They came and got my keys and went into my apartment and clean the floor. I had a bad feel about allowing them to go into the apartment to clean up for me. But I did let them inside, my place, I went back to my place later that week, to cleaning up my apartment to move out, because I couldn't afforded to pay 800.00 by myself. I go into my fathers room and remember all the things he had told me about his life when he was a little boy. When he was living how he was saying in the light with the window open he could see a little boy standing, in the living room calling him. I would look and try to see what he was looking at. But never could see the little boy at all. This was happening a lot with in the four months he was here on earth, I knew it was close he was on oxygen at night and starting to see things around the home. He talked about talking to family and friends before it was too late. I knew it was getting close before his last days had come on this earth. I think about him often and I know he is watching over me because we had a close bond, that is what I remember the most, and his laugh, and the way he would charm women and they would melt like butter when he talked to them.

I have forgiveness in my heart about all the wrong that I have had to endure in my life. I want to have a wonderful life with good friends and family around. With out the drama and problems that I have see in the pass, I feel it is important to live a stress free life as much as possible. This is my desire to have for myself in life, with Gods help I can have it for myself

First Father pass away

The Father that I never knew pass away during the time of my first divorce. In 1996-1997. that he pass way before I could ever meet him, it upset me so much that I thought I was cheated out of every getting to know him, I did not know this until 2007 when I started looking into this man life. He was in the army, very hard worker, he probably love life had a passion for food, and the restaurant business. Some one would bring food from his restaurant for us to eat on Sundays. I never talk to him ever But I do remember thinking some one is watching me all the time. That's how I felt growing up as if there were eyes on me always. You know the feeling you get inside, when you feel something has your hair on the back of your neck standing up. That is how I felt growing up. I know now what it was it was his eyes on me, watching from a distance and helping me with food and things. I was not told by any one their, put with Gods perfect timing things become unfolding before my eyes. I like to say what is done in the dark, shall come to the like. You shall see the truth for yourself, and you will be victorious over it. This is my truth and I have learn a lot about myself. My biological father miss out on my conversation, happy thought, grandchild, and all the positive things in life, getting to know me as a person who, has dreams and ambitions in life, He could given me father and daughter advice about men, and finding the right man to married. How to manage money, what the best car to buy, how to care for a car, If he did not want me that okay to, because this was a love affair between two people who were married to someone else. It happened I am here, I need to make the best of it and move on with life, and be happy in all things in life. I only want to know about him because of my children, and grandchildren. who have a 50% chance of getting ataxia 5. as they grow older and get into their 50's and older. I want this to be my legacy of my life as to my purpose in life and why I was here, to spread the good news about Christ, and to be a role model for others, to show that if you have a disability, life is not over, it just beginning, and should not give up on your dreams, of being happy and have a blessed life you can have it. I Think having a disability should not stop a person in doing what you can do for one self, on your own level and skills that you have. My disability has changed my life in the way I do things I have to think it through before I do it. I try to figure out the ends and out of things, that I need to get done. I have a positive out look on life, this kind of thinking helps me to keep moving, and not let my ataxia win, and take over my life. For my grandchildren all 7 of them to know how their grandmother wrote this book for them to remember her by, as act of love to share with their families and friends. Don't' be discourage, keep on working in your school work, and trust God to guide you and keep you, is my prayer for my grandchildren. Like the song says I know the Lord will make a way yes he will. This is what we speak in times of trials in our lives, and all the time. So grandchildren remember God will make away for you if you believe him. Do great things for God, and be kind to one another, love unconditional, respect all adult figures in your life. You will be blessed, Don't forget to honor your parents. Remembrance of all your grandparents and your great grandparents that came before, and paved the way for you to be in United States of American.

Experience

My life experience that impact me the most and give me the light bulb moment was when I had lost all my balance, could not walk one foot in front of they other. I did not know what had happen to me or Why it happened to me? I just knew at that moment something had gone wrong in my body. We move to a big city with no close family around, and I am in this big hospital talking to family on the phone in hospital room. I felt like I was alone in this place my family member had to work.

When my family member went to jail and my car was impounded by the police department. This made me feel like I did not make a very good choice in life. I did not listen to anyone, about being apart of that environment, did the opposite of what I was suppose to do. That is what to get when you do not listen to an elder.

Trying to help someone who will not listen to me about things, that could help them. Just have to leave them alone, for them to figure it out for themselves. My experience helping in my church or my community is a blessing that I can do it at the level that I know I can handle, without over doing it.

Living with family has been a very interesting experience for me, I get to know the good and the bad of living with family members. They may not want to pay for bills, or may not feel like picking up. I think every family, has something like that going on.

When I became a mother of two sons, they have touch my heart in such a positive way, I would protect them as much as I could. They were my gifts to the world, with their cool control of there soul and mind, I could try to be more calm and control like them, I am still working on that part of being calm.

Loosing 2 babies was hard for me to handle, not a day goes by I don't think about them. I carry them in my heart and soul and, I will see them in heaven one day. This happened to me because I was trying to please a family member, so I went along with it and they abortion one with out drugs and another with drugs, this was very painful in my body and my spirit it hurt so much, I cried over this for long time. The one with drugs I did not feel anything with that one, with out drugs you could feel it being taken out of your body, it was very painful and it upset me so very much. I was hurt, and upset with myself about it. I told myself that I would not do this again for no one every again. I did care who that person was, I don't recommend this to anyone at all. This is a choice you would have to make and pray over before you do such a thing. In the 1980's We did not go to church, hardly at all, so it was the way we lived then. Now I feel it is not the right thing to do, and there is other choices you can make in life, beside having abortion. When you are young and trying to please others, you make many mistakes in life. This experience save my left eye, It was a cornea transplant that I had to have in 1989-1990 my left eye start to have a scar line in the middle of the cornea and was going to lose my vision in that one eye. I was sent to a eye specialist at the eye institution where I live. After their did all their examinations, they said I had to have a cornea transplant. My next step was to get myself put on a waiting list for a donor list for a cornea. I was put on the list on January of 1990 and wait until May 20, 1990 to have my transplant done. The way they did it was some one passed away from a car accident that was a match to me. They tell you to be ready, because they can call you anytime to come in and have your surgery done. On that morning of May 20, at 6:00 a.m. They called and off I went to the hospital for my transplant to be done on my eye. I get their and register and prepare me for my surgery. They hook me up to monitor my blood pressure, heart rate they give me a shot in my eye to get me ready for my transplant they put me to sleep. While I am sleeping I here music playing and people talking as there doing my surgery on my left eye. I cant make out what they are saying just a lot of noise. The surgery was a success I have a patch on my eyes and a lot of drops to put into my eyes and doctors appointment to go to for several months. The drops are for me to use to make use my cornea is taking in my eye and does not become infected and rejection in my eye. I had special glasses made after my surgery, and special contact lenses to wear after a year or so. We all should become a donor so we can save someone like this person did for me. Saving my eye so I could see out of it. I want to thank the family for doing what they did for me. It has helped me a lot with my seeing how to get around. Basic things that people take for granted. Like seeing the trees, birds, and the flowers that come in the spring time. It is wonderful to be a donor, I am one also, to save some who is in need of it so much, and you can help that person if you match there blood or system. How ever they figure how to match that person, with a special test. You could give some one life, and a chance for happiness by being a donor of organs.

My experience with my parent has been a hard one, painful, tearful, homeless, sad, loneliness and rough since 2010 when she said that she did not want my gift that I was giving on birthday, I was told to keep the gift. I gave it away and did not call or come around to visit anymore, I was trying to have a relationship with my parent. I felt she wanted nothing to do with me, so I left the parent alone. I could not get. the answer to my question, on who my father was. It is 2015 and thinking about calling the parent to wish Happy Easter Sunday. That would be a surprise to the parent If I did do that. I hope my parent picks up the phone and talks to me, I heard that parent is different in her spirit and soul, we shall see if that is true. For example parent celebrated 70 years of life, we were their for the celebration, but not included in the flower placing on the table, or any of the traditions that came with it. We sit in the back in the corner away from the main table, like we did not have a mother at all it was just that one side of the family that was giving the cerebration of life party. We did not get our names called or acknowledgment, both of us were saying things about like their not the oldest, why did they not includes us in honoring our parent. The sister, and cousins, brother all the guest that knew us had their heads looking down at the table, as if they were ashamed to look up at us. We talk through the whole cerebration of life party, but no one knew, we saying smart things and we did not know we were on the DVD, until the family member quickly took out the DVD and inserted into the DVD player than we realized we were on the DVD talking smart about our family members. All the relatives and friends that had their heads down, were laugh and smiling at what we were saying. They other family members went into another room and closed the door upset. This is how we were treated all our lives, always feeling second best, to the other siblings in the family. That why if my parent did not want my gift that was okay with me. I was never valued in this family, in the first place. I was just there to work for them, and take care of the smaller children. I think I had one on one time with my parent at least one time. That when you go and have a special time with parent, doing fun things together. If I did have more fun times I don't' recall them.

I remember coming to my parent for a place to stay while I was going through my divorce, parent told me I could stay one night, and I had to go back in the morning, to where I came from. I could not stay a few days with them. I needed my parent, I was told, no one told you to married that person, you go back and deal with it. So I packed up my sons, and went back to where I came from broken heart ed, and feeling low, and not loved, by the parent again. After my 16 year marriage was ending and wanted some time to heal my broken heart. I was sent back to my sad life, to work it out for myself with out my parents help. I am told this parent is different know, I have to see it first before I believe it. Anything is possible for a person to change their ways, and be different if they, want to change the way they use to be, they can.

I have not spoken to my parent for a long time. I know we are suppose to be family, but how much pain does one have to take before it is enough? Do you keep opening, up your heart for more pain and sadness, and mistreatment, to get your parent to even care about you. Life is to short for all that to be around all the time. I want to enjoy life and what it has to offer, we are but a short time I want it to be filled with love and kindness for one another, and not hate for your family members. This experience scared myself and another sibling, one night my younger sibling was upset with with the boyfriend because he told him something that was not nice. The sibling came in to the kitchen, which it was not our turn to do the dishes, we were doing dishes, the sibling grabbed the knife, we were holding the sibling and pushing against wall and got the knife from sibling, yelling for the other parent to come, while the other parent, is talking not noticing what is going on in the kitchen with the knife. That sibling had anger in his heart towards the parent, and was going to use that knife on him. The parent took him and talk to sibling in the other room. The sibling was sent to live with other family members for when he was in high school.

That sibling has been living away from home for along time. This was not a good place to live as a child, that sibling is adult know, and that parent has pass away. If parent promise to care for those siblings more than the rest of us. It has show for many years of my life, it has been favoritism with them for years. We take five steps forward and tens steps backward while living at home.

When I was in band with my other sibling we had to raise money to go to England. So I would put my candy in the locker to sell it at lunch or break time. I did this with about 3 or 4 boxes of candy. I sold all of my candies, to my surprise my sibling took it home and the parent paid for it. The parent went and told the band teacher, to not let me go to England, they allowed they other child to go, and I had to stay home and, here about her trip to England. The band teacher was not happy, with that put that is what happened to me. I raised the money to go, put was taken out, and replaced with another family member. This was in high school I was so upset with everyone, about that it hurt my heart to know that I worked hard to go out and sell my candies and did not get to go at all. That sibling did not do anything to raise money, to go England but took what I sold and add to the box candies that the parent purchase. You know when you are a kid and you want a special toys, this is how I felt about going to England at that time. I was excited happy and wanted to jump for joy about going to England. One day I will be able to go to England to see all the things that they have to offer, may be even meeting the Queen of England. That would be the best gift I could give myself is that trip to England. I want to see the changing of the guard at the at the queens home. Taste the food, and see all the museums, with their rich history. Feel what it is like, and be apart of the culture, and see all that it has to offer. Attend church in England and see God's work in England. All over that area. Be blessed their and feel Gods love, their compassion, for his people.

I have Learned

I have learn that what is done in the dark shall come to the light. If you think you are getting away with a lie it will find you, and the truth will come out, from behind a tree and get you. Not everything is what it seams to be in life. We all make mistakes as we go in life. And not our place to judge anyone about their pass or present life issue. Just be honesty no matter how hard it maybe to tell the truth about a issue in your life. It will come out at the end. It maybe 50 years from know, but it will come out. And you will still have to face the music about that issue that you have been hiding all your life. I have learned that forgiving that person frees you from all the pain, and sorrow, anger, mistreatment, name calling, evil that was done to you all those years of your life. You can smile and be happy and have love for your family and friends that have done you wrong all these years. You set example for your children to see and copy as they grow up in this life. If you walking around without forgiveness in your heart they will also see you doing that and copy what you are doing. Life is too short to hold on to all this bitterness in your heart. I have learn all this had to happened to make me a strong women of God, and to show me that everything that is said by other people is not the truth, and to listen to what people say as the truth about a issue that is going on in your life. If I would of took the time to listen to what the elders were saying about things in my life that were true I would of known the truth. Be aware of what is said and listen, to people when say the truth it is. My parent maybe embarrassed about the pass, but time will heal the pain of it all, some day they will speak about that very issue. And then they may carry it to the grave and not say a word to any one at all.

I have learn to speak for myself and to go out and get what I want out of life, for myself and my family. To have courage and not give my power to others in life, if you don't like my weight they your not my friend or mate, this is who I am, before I would try to please people not anymore, this is what you see is what you get. If this is not good enough, they move on, and I will keep on going with life. I have learn to trust God about the issues in my life as I speak that God will work them out for his glory and not for my glory. Have great self value of your self, I did not value myself in my life like I do now. I feel I am a great women and worthy of all the good things of life and husband who values, me and family, that loves me for who I am, there is no one at this present moment only time will tell the story. God knows who that person is.

I have learn to listen to your inner voice about a problem or issue that you don't feel comfortable about. Follow your inner man about what you are feeling, and most of the time you will be right about that issue that you feel uncomfortable about. Learn to read body language I have to work on that because I use to believe everything some one would tell me. I would find out that it is a lie and they stand in front of me and tell me a lie to believe. I find out from a family member that its a big fat lie later on, I would be telling them about what was said. The family member would tell me the truth. Writing this book has shown me that my health has improved and God has given me the strength to look at my life. It not all bad, there was some good in it, and some polishing of some rough edges that had to be done. I have learn to be humble and polite to all who are in my presence, to treat everyone with respect, and kindness, be honest and genuine to all. I have learned from writing about my life, is you can't make a parent love you, They have to want to love you from their own heart, Buying their love will not make them love you anymore than the next person, they will take the gift and keep on moving.

I thought maybe if I do this or do that parent would love me. If that is how she feels you leave that person alone. People come and go in your life, family is suppose to be with you forever, that is not the case in this family. Some family members want you out of the family, and removed from the family by mistreating, bulling, saying hurtful things, and still want you to come around so you can be mistreated again. That is not a very nice thing to be apart of.

I choose to stay away from it all, and live in peace and joy and happiness. Life is too short to live in drama all the time, and worry if you said the wrong thing to upset some one in the family. I have learn to stand up for myself and to trust God to fight my battles and work it out for me. Life is not always easy. It is learning from the lesson, or storm, that I am going through at this time of my life. I had to learn to speak up for myself, and do it with grace and peace and a soft voice and still be heard. I am not perfect I have had plenty of struggles, with walking, speaking, ataxia 5, not want to keep my balance money problems. This all part of life, I make it through all of it, and I am still here. I have learn to be around positive people, and up lift myself when I feel down about life, or feel bad about things that go wrong. We all have the good and the bad and the ugly happened to us. How we handle it makes a difference in our lives, we can not blame they other person for it. We have too look in the mirror at ourselves and take responsibility for it. I learned that God has away of working it out for his glory, I give it all to him, and thanks him for getting me through all the trails and pain of life. He brought me out on they other side of the mountain, to a place where peace and joy are and love in my heart, it was not easy to get to this point in my life, but God did it all. I am walking around on my own power, and loving that I can do that, 6 years ago I was using a walker to get around, but God work this out for me to move, I thank him every day that I can walk, and talk. I help family member who using my walker that she bought from me for someone else to use. She needs it for herself to get around to help her walk. I have learn to keep on trusting in God no matter what you feel is wrong in your life. He is the only thing that stays the same, everything changes around us.

I have learned to smile when your heart is hurting, and family members decided to keep life changing secrets from me. All of it comes out in the end anyway. All the lies, dishonesty all comes out at the end, why not just tell the truth. I learned that life is too short to live in lies and dishonesty, how is it going to help me in the long run, to live in lies and dishonesty. One lie leads to another lie and another, it will keep going. I learned the truth will come out even if it is 100 years from now. I learn that people can change it they want to, and be a different person, with a better mind set they start with.

I have learn to forgive since I had written this book, I feel God will forgive me if I said anything that is not pleasing, about my family members, or hurt anyone feelings, in my writing about what I have been feeling in my heart about my life and my journey on this earth the short 58 years of life that I have lived. I was afraid to write what I was feeling about my life on this earth, for fear of hurting others all these years. If feels good to talk about myself, and speak from my heart about my struggles, and pains that I have been through. I though I was done, because of my ataxia 5, it turns out I not done, God has shown me his will and his grace to keep on going and finish my race. I want readers to know that you can have health issues and still make a difference in this world that we live, Don't count yourself short in life. I have battled my fears of writing what I have felt for years in my heart, and may not have all the answer, but I am a work in progress still. I learned to please God and not man all the time, to do what is pleasing for God and not try to please people like I have been doing for many years of my life. I have learned a long time ago, that I don't' have to fight any battles, just give it to God he will fight them for me. I have learned that forgives is free, it helps you not have hate in your heart towards that person, that did you wrong. You can sleep at night, not trying to get even with someone, who did you wrong in life. That is what I am trying to achieve in my life, with honesty with all that I say or do for me in my life. This is the best thing I could do for myself, at this time as reaching my next level of life going to my young age of 59 in November. I am able to see ways to make life better for me. If it is Gods will I will make it to see my 59 and then my 60 birthday. But God allow me to do it with grace and joy and love in my heart to speak what was on my heart, to talk about my life, as a kid and adult women.

The Ending

This writing journey has been very eye, opening for me and interesting, experience for me. I have learned about myself. I have learn that I have been trying to please other people and not think about myself and my feelings about what is going. I cant help everyone out, we all make choices in life and have to live with our choices, if it is a good or bad decision it out there it made. I have a trusting heart and believe what people tell me as truth, when it could be a lie.

I did not want to write this book, because I was afraid of what I was going to find out about myself. I have been a people pleas-er all my life, It time to stand up for myself and be heard. I learned this kind of behavior from my home life as a kid growing up in this dysfunctional family that I was apart of. I saw myself weak, and intimidated my family members for a long time, who thought they had the power over me. As the years have gone by, it has changed and I feel strong, with courage and power to speak for myself about things that are important to me. When you become older your thinking changes, you don't care what people think, it about what you think, and how you feel. Sometimes it time for a change in your life, and to move forward with life. God has help me with the my issue of being a people pleas er, I have learned not to do as much, but to think first before I do it, and to think is that the right thing to do. It took me awhile to be able to say no to people in my family, and friends if I can't do something. God has help me to speak and walk and hold back on people pleasing.

To be kind and loving to others, and their feelings and their issues. I wanted this book to be a positive true story of a girl who went through a lot to get to where she is today. Make this a positive and not a negative thing, I did all my own writing, no one wrote the words of my book, I did it without help from anyone. I did not think I could write a book at all, until I tried and worked at it every day. Until I think I am done writing my thoughts on paper, the I will stop.

You may think your problem is more important than other people, who have hunger, poor living condition, and sickness around them, and the lack of money, to help them. There is always going to be some one worse off they yourself, so be thankful for life and the problems we have here, if we lived in another county it could be worse. Keep those positive thoughts going for yourself and, do something nice for someone else.

What you go through in life does not make you a bad person at all, it the choices you make that may get you into trouble. The only thing you can do is forgive yourselves and others it you have said or done anything to hurt someone. Forgive yourself for what you have done in life, and keep on moving on to reach your goals.

Yes I have many challenges in my life, but with the grace of God and my family that help me through the bad times of my life, when God was caring me through them. I was able to get up from the lost of my balance and walk around with my illness, as a blessed child of God. I was able to get back up again, you too can get back up again, and keep on trying. It not over yet.

I am a happy women today from all my pass life lesson that I have been through It has taught me to be here in the moment as a human being and enjoy life to it fullest. Never judge anyone, because you don't t know what there life lesson is are was. Be friendly if you want friends and have a positive out look on life at all times. Just because you had a bad beginning dose not mean have a bad ending. Life gives us many challenges and hurtles to go over to get to they other side of the track. There maybe more to come in the book writing business for me later on in life. We shall she what the future holds for me as a writer.

www.ingramcontent.com/pod-product-compliance
Ingram Content Group UK Ltd.
Pitfield, Milton Keynes, MK11 3LW, UK
UKHW041914190726
13854UKWH00003B/1243